FIND
YOUR
PEACE

FIND
YOUR
BALANCE

CELEBRATE
YOURSELF
TODAY

CHOOSE
JOY
DAILY

NURTURE
YOUR
SOUL

EMPOWER
YOURSELF
DAILY

EMBRACE
YOUR
INNER
STRENGTH

LOVE
YOUR
BODY

BE KIND
TO
YOURSELF

1

BREATHE
AND LET
GO

TRUST THE
JOURNEY

YOU
DESERVE
HAPPINESS

1

SAVOR
SMALL
MOMENTS

LIVE IN
GRATITUDE

CELEBRATE
YOUR
PROGRESS

BELIEVE IN
YOURSELF

OWN
YOUR
STORY

YOU ARE
WORTHY

YOU ARE
ENOUGH

RADIATE
POSITIVE
ENERGY

PRIORITIZE
SELF-CARE

CHERISH
SISTER
FRIENDS

FOCUS ON
THE
PRESENT

BE YOUR
BEST
FRIEND

FOLLOW
YOUR
DREAMS